About this book

Many children have difficulty puzzling out letters because they
are abstract symbols. Letterland's worldwide success is all about its
enduring characters who give these symbols life and stop them from
being abstract. In this book we meet Robber Red. His story is carefully
designed to emphasise the sounds that the letter 'R' makes in words.
This definitive, original story book is an instant collector's classic,
making learning fun for a new generation of readers.

A TEMPLAR BOOK

This edition published in the UK in 2008 by Templar Publishing
an imprint of The Templar Company plc,
The Granary, North Street, Dorking, Surrey, RH4 1DN, UK
www.templarco.co.uk

First published by Hamlyn Publishing, 1985
Devised and produced by The Templar Company plc

ISBN 978-1-84011-786-8

Printed in China

Classic LETTERLAND
Storybooks

Robber Red
and the Robot

Written by
Vivien Stone & Lyn Wendon

Illustrated by
Jane Launchbury

templar publishing

Robber Red was feeling cross. All day he had searched for things to rob, but he could not find anything.

As he ran back to his hide-out, empty-handed, he nearly tripped over some bits of metal lying by the road.

Robber Red stopped and looked at them. "They will never make me rich," he thought. "But maybe I could make something with them."

So he picked up all the bits of metal and ran the rest of the way home.

Back in his hide-out, Robber Red had a really good idea. "I know," he cried, I'll make a metal robot. Then it can do all my robbing for me!" So he set to work.

All night long Robber Red hammered the bits of metal together. Soon his robot was nearly ready. On its chest he put three red buttons.
The first button said RUN.
The second button said ROB.
The third button said RETURN.

Robber Red pressed the RUN button to see if it worked. His robot ran around perfectly. Then he pressed all three buttons. The robot raced off like a rocket.

Robber Red was so excited that he could hardly wait for his robot to return. "If my robot can rob as well as he can run, I'm going to be rich, rich, rich!" he cried.

Soon his robot came racing back. In its hand was... a radio! "Grrreat!" growled Robber Red, and he hid the radio in a secret room in his hide-out.

He pressed the buttons again and off went the robot, racing down the road. Soon it was back... this time with a bright red ruby ring. How the ring sparkled in the sunshine! "Remarkable!" thought Robber Red. "This robot is better at robbing than I am!"

Before long Robber Red's secret room was full of things his robot had robbed from people all over Letterland. There were radios and rulers, roller skates and reading books, not to mention the Quarrelsome Queen's very own ruby ring!

Robber Red ran round and round with delight. "My robot will make me rich, rich, rich!" he shouted.

Every day Robber Red sent his robot out to rob. His secret room grew fuller and fuller. But the people in Letterland were very unhappy. "We must stop the robot!" they cried. So they held a meeting.

Nearly everyone from Letterland was there. "Stop the robot from robbing," they cried angrily. But nobody knew how.

Then Mr I had an idea. "First," he said, "we must stop the robot from running. Then he won't be able to rob us any more."

"Just leave it to me," said Fireman Fred. "I will catch this rascal."

The next morning, Fireman Fred hid behind a bush by the road to Robber Red's hide-out. He waited for the robot to appear.

Soon it came rushing down the road, on its way to rob some breakfast rolls from the castle kitchen.

Just as the robot was about to run past, Fireman Fred popped up from behind the bush, and sprayed foam from his hose all over the road.

The robot slipped and slithered. Then crash! It fell over, flat on its back!

Soon everyone was crowding round. "We've got him," they cried. "Well done Fireman Fred." "But now what do we do with him?" asked Dippy Duck.

"Let Eddy Elephant squirt water over him," shouted Quarrelsome Queen. "That will make him too rusty to run." "No, that's not right," said the Hairy Hat Man. "The best way to stop him robbing is to re-program him!"

"But how?" cried Dippy Duck. "I know," said Clever Cat. "Let's remove the ROB button and see what happens." So Ticking Tom fetched his tool box and the re-programming began.

Ticking Tom removed the red ROB button very carefully and put some tape over the hole. Then he put the robot back on its feet again. It stood there smiling happily.

"Now what?" asked Bouncy Ben. "We can't just leave him here or Robber Red will find him."

"I think I know," said Clever Cat and she gently pushed the RETURN button with her paw. Right away the robot raced off up the road the way he had come.

"Where's he going?" they all cried. Clever Cat smiled knowingly. "We'll just have to wait and see," she said.

Meanwhile, Robber Red was getting very annoyed. "Where can that robot be?" he growled.

Suddenly he saw the robot running up the road... but it was empty-handed.

"Why haven't you robbed anything?" shouted Robber Red angrily.

But the robot didn't reply. Instead, it rushed right past him and into the hide-out.

Before Robber Red could even blink, the robot had grabbed everything from the secret room.

It took the radios and rulers. It took the roller skates and reading books, and even the ruby ring. Then off it ran back down the road.

Robber Red turned bright red with rage when he realised what was happening. The robot was returning everything to its rightful owner!

"**G**rrr" roared Robber Red.
"They've ruined my robot.
Now I'll never be rich!" and he
roared so loud that everyone in
Letterland could hear him.

"He's really in a rage," they said,
as the robot ran round giving
everything back.

"His robot will never rob anyone
again," said Ticking Tom.
"Now all we need to do is think of a
really good way to re-program
Robber Red!"

THE END